Exploring Happiness

Anish R Gaddam

For the Ones Who Wish to Experience the Greatness of Life

EXPLORING HAPPINESS

Copyright © 2024 by Anish Gaddam

All rights reserved.

No portion of this book may be reproduced in any form – except as permitted by U.S. copyright law – without written permission from the author.

Contact for Permission: [ARG@EverlastingPublishers.com]

This publication is designed to provide accurate and authoritative information in regard to the subject matter covered. While the author has used their best efforts to ensure the content's accuracy and completeness, they make no representations or warranties with respect to the accuracy or completeness of the contents of this book and disclaim any implied warranties regarding its suitability for specific situations. It is advised to consult a professional when appropriate.

The author is not liable for any loss of profit or any other commercial damages, including but not limited to special, incidental, consequential, personal, or other damages.

All brand names and product names used in this book are trademarks or trade names of their respective holders.

To my younger self and future self, whom I aim to do right by

Table of Contents

Chapter 1: Happiness Explained	1
Chapter 2: Physical Happiness	13
Chapter 3: Mental Happiness	41
Chapter 4: Sustainable Happiness	73
Chapter 5: A Personal Anecdote	97
Chapter 6: A Daily Life	107
Chapter 7: Ending Remarks	115
Cited Works	121

Chapter 1

Happiness Explained

Happiness. One emotion that encompasses the entirety of human existence. One emotion that controls all the others. One emotion that determines our view of life.

An emotion all humans on this vast planet constantly chase after. An ever-present desire to experience a greater possibility within our lives. An emotion that conveys a profound sense of being. A profound sense of security. And a profound sense of peace.

An emotion we pursue in al that we do – from the work we undertake to the family we take charge of – whether that be in pursuit of it for ourselves or others.

An emotion that we sometimes feel and sometimes detach from. Sometimes see and sometimes are blind to. Sometimes hear and sometimes are deaf of. But an emotion we seek nonetheless.

Whether it is the poorest of poor laborer trying to pave their path, or the richest of rich tycoon aspiring to advance global control, all man is on the quest of seeking to experience or produce happiness.

Happiness is truly the only emotion that exists in the entirety of the world. What is sadness but the absence of happiness? What is anger but a pinnacle absence of happiness coupled with distaste? What is peace but a blissful experience of happiness? What is fear but a lack of happiness blended with uncertainty? What is love but happiness incarnate and exemplified?

Let me provide an example. Let's say you recently applied to your dream job, but got an email today saying you were not selected. You would likely be feeling 'sad' and 'depressed'. But you are not 'sad' because you did not get the job. Rather, you are unhappy because you did not experience the happiness that would have come with getting the job.

Every proclaimed human emotion can be tied back to either experiencing or not experiencing happiness.

But what actually is happiness? The dictionary definition calls it a state of well-being and contentment.[1] In simple words, it is our response to feeling good – characterized by smiles, laughter, warm feelings and other feel-good reactions.

Some may experience it most by partying with friends and going out. Others may encounter it by taking time for themselves and catering to their needs.

But one common factor among all beings on this planet is the feature that happiness is **always within**.

Yes, one's lifestyle can cause them happiness. Yes, one's occupation can cause them to be happy. Yes, one's achievements can bring joy.

But happiness is always the product of the processes inside our mind. Happiness or lack of happiness is the consequence of our reaction to all the events and experiences we come across in our life.

'Happiness depends upon ourselves'

Aristotle

Happiness is something we have full authority over. We choose how we respond to all that occurs in our life, whether that be an inherently positive or negative reaction.

Take this scenario for example. Imagine if I called you a worthless, lame loser. Pretty insulting right? But imagine if I instead said "dunnapothu lagga kanipistunnāvu ra." All my Telugu people reading this are gasping right now. But, for those of that do not understand Telugu, we have absolutely no clue what was said/written. We are probably trying to look up a translation to see what this actually means (trust me, it's not accurate).

The second statement that was written is far more insulting and demeaning than the first. But, because we may not understand the language it was written in, it has absolutely no effect on us. For all we know, it could have talked about anything from the fact that we look like Scarlett Johansson or Tom Cruise all the way to Michigan State's loss to Michigan on October 26th, 2024 (GO BLUE!).

The meaning behind this is that we are all in control of how anything in life affects us. We choose whether or not any event – good or bad – will change the way we respond or behave.

Words are nothing but words. Our emotions are simply our reactions to all these words around us. If we control how words affect us, we can control our emotions. And when we control our emotions, we can cause ourselves to experience, during every moment of every day, nothing but the one true emotion: happiness.

But I want to make something clear. Emotional control has nothing to do with suppressing feelings. It simply has to do with choice.

Take this example. Let's say you are having a truly unfortunate day. You woke up late for work. Didn't eat anything. Got your car towed. Your pet fish died. Got a ticket just after getting your car back. And, at the end of all that, found out that you weren't selected for a promotion at work. By the time this last event happened, you would probably be laughing out of disbelief. You may not necessarily be happy, but you want to avoid dealing with the various situations so much that you just choose to ignore them and carry on.

And that is all emotional control is: choosing not to deal. Choose to avoid grappling with any and all feelings that may cause you to be unhappy or negative.

Please note, this does not mean we should avoid doing things that may cause negative feelings. In fact, it is often through doing that which makes us suffer that we ultimately come out stronger.

The trick here is to just avoid dealing with all the feelings that aim to bring us down. Do the hard stuff. Don't feel the hard feelings.

This may seem heartless. Like why would you ever want to limit your feelings? And the truth is, we shouldn't. The more we feel, the more human we become.

But the fact of the matter is, most of us will avoid doing what we know we need to do simply because we feel it may be hard or make us feel uncomfortable.

And this is what is wrong. If we could do all that we must do while still keeping all of our feelings intact, whether happy, stressed, uncomfortable or embarrassed, then that would be the optimal resolution. But because we as humans are wired to run away from difficult-to-handle feelings, the realistic solution is to simply block them out in order to stay headstrong on our path.

Some people make the argument that they are neither sad nor happy. But that is simply not true. I am telling you. If we are not happy, then we are unhappy – experiencing a lack of happiness. But that is not how we humans are meant to live!

I want you to recall the last time you felt absolutely ecstatic – whether it was recently or in childhood.

Wasn't it among the more blissful feelings you have experienced in your life? Didn't it make you forget the so-called 'worries' of the day and simply **BE** in the moment? And, if it was at work, didn't it make you work that much more effectively, efficiently and smoothly?

The reason why all these statements are true is because **happiness** is all we as humans are constantly supposed to **feel, experience and express**. For it elevates us to the peaks of our existence, in all aspects.

'We Hold These Truths to Be Self-Evident, That All Men Are Created Equal, That They Are Endowed by Their Creator with Certain Unalienable Rights, That Among These Are Life, Liberty and The Pursuit of Happiness'

the Committee of Five

Regardless of what faith you believe in – Christianity, Islam, Hinduism, Judaism, Buddhism, Sikhism, Jainism, independent, atheist or other – the times that we feel closest to the 'all-powerful' are when we are in a state of ecstatic happiness.

This is because the forces of the universe are dominant in such a way that **happiness** brings us closer to our most **conscious and spiritual selves.**

Take a look at this:

If you are religious, what is one of the first things we do during good times? We smile and pray. What is one of the first things we do during bad times? We frown and pray for better times.

If you are non-religious, what is one of first things we do during good times? We smile and are joyous. What is one of the first things we do during bad times? We frown and wish for better times.

No matter the situation, humans are wired to always strive for good times. I am very confident that nobody reading this book is unhappy during 'good' times.

We associate good times with happiness and bad times with unhappiness. The happier we are, the better we think the time is. The unhappier we are, the worse we think the time is.

At all times, our system is programmed to always **crave** for and **strive to live** in good times and savor the subsequent happiness.

We associate happiness with a smile and unhappiness with a frown. Smiling is most natural to us. Frowning is not. There is a reason why smiling takes less than half of the facial muscles to do than frowning.[2] It is also why, after a long time of frowning, we have to ease our face as it becomes tense – often times doing so by putting on a smile.

A smile is all we must constantly display. The more we physically smile, the happier we will subconsciously begin to feel. The happier we are subconsciously, the more consciously we begin to experience it.

So, kick-start the cycle of happiness. *Simply Smile!*

'A gentle word, a kind look, a good-natured smile can work wonders and accomplish miracles'

William Hazlitt

Chapter 2

Physical Happiness

So far, we have explored the essence of what happiness truly is. But how can we actually go about endlessly experiencing it in our lives?

There are two significant paths to happiness. One is the physical road; altering what we do with our body to receive and experience greater happiness. The other is the mental road, entailing the mastery of our mindset and states of mind to produce happiness.

This chapter overviews the physical path.

In changing the physical aspects of one's life in order to tailor towards happiness, there are four main workable elements: eating, sleeping, exercising and moving.

EATING

Depression. Anxiety. Anger. Sadness. What is the single most prevalent factor among all these 'emotional' states-of-being? It is vitamin and nutrient deficiency.

About one century ago, our planet's soil was so rich that the nutrients fruits and vegetables provided would support mankind even if eaten in small quantities.

When substances like nitrogen were first introduced into the ground, farmers were stunned to see their crops blossom like never before. And so, we kept adding and adding and adding these substances as we needed them.

Today, we are dispensing significantly more man-made 'organic' elements into crops to achieve the **SAME** results as we were in earlier years. Why is that?

It is because our man-made technologies are no match for the intricate systems of Mother Nature. And our misplaced confidence in our conduct has led to practices such as over-farming, mass-production farming and excessive use of 'organic' fertilizers – measures which are depleting our food supply faster than ever before and diminishing crop nutritional content just as quickly.

In the early 20th century, the density of nutrients a single orange provided is equivalent to that which eight oranges provide today.[1] This decline in the organic nutrient content of food is a significant factor contributing to the widespread lack of happiness experienced by many people today.

Eating is not about the consumption of food. It is about the content received from food that binds to our body, influencing our energy, hormones and overall health.

Food is simply the intake of protein, carbs, lipids (fats), vitamins, minerals and water. Out of all these, a crucial, and often forgotten, element to focus on is vitamins.

The goal of eating is to gain energy – energy which enables us to do what we want throughout the day. Currently, most of us are probably sticking to a traditional food pyramid diet, which says get X amount of Carbs, X amount of protein and X amount of fats from fruits, veggies, meats, etc.

But the truth is, getting a sufficient quantity of food from each of these groups is simply not enough – we must support them with processes that produce energy from that food. The main process is metabolism.

Vitamins are what support nutrients received from food endure these bodily processes that result in the production of energy.

The vitamins we should focus on are vitamin B, vitamin C and vitamin D. Each of these is crucial for supporting various body functions. B vitamins aid in the conversion of food into usable cellular energy through metabolism.[2] Vitamin C helps maintain a healthy immune system,[3] which, when functioning well, uses less energy to protect the body, leaving more energy available for daily activities. Vitamin D supports proper bone health and reduces inflammation,[4] which, in turn, makes us physically stronger and less susceptible to injuries or strain that could drain our energy levels.

But what is more important than getting these vitamins is where we get them from. Consider this example:

When we fill our gas, we may put 87, 89, 91 or 93 octane based on what our engine takes. If you ever input the wrong octane rated fuel, you will notice various side effects. Your car may get less gas mileage. Your engine may stutter and run less efficient. You may put too high of an octane and hurt your wallet. And so on.

So, there is a just right amount of burning capacity that makes the fuel suitable for our car.

Similarly, the human body has its own fuel: food. And for us, the food that is most optimal is that which goes in and out of the system the easiest and fastest, as our metabolite processes will be most capable and efficient.

For us, this fuel that burns the fastest is fruits. We should aim to have a diet composing of at least 30% fruits. Eating a higher ratio of fruits compared with other foods will allow our body to digest the other non-fruit food faster and with less residue, allowing our bodies to stay at peak performance.

Connecting this with our vitamin needs, we should be eating ample apples, bananas, oranges, kiwis, watermelon and cantaloupe. Each of these has potent amounts of various vitamins that will combine to bring our body to a high-performance capability. And, they taste so darn good!

Of course, eating all of these may be difficult daily and burdensome financially. So, if you have to focus on just one, eat oranges. Oranges contain B vitamins and vitamin C, and are by far the best fuel for us.

It is especially important to eat ample fruits and vegetables when we eat processed foods and high amounts of meat. Fish stays in the body for 6 hours, chicken for 12 hours, beef for 24 hours and pork for 48 hours. Similarly, processed food is significantly harder for our bodies to pass through than nature-provided food.

So, to counteract the difficulty of digestion of these foods, sticking to a balanced diet full of vitamin-rich fruits and veggies (particularly fruits) can prove especially beneficial.

But food is not the sole provider of vitamins and well-being. Nature and activity are some of the best providers.

The sun provides more vitamin D than we need. Running helps increase our absorption of vitamin B. Yoga supports vitamin B utilization. Dance and physically moving hobbies support functions of vitamin B.

Integrate such activities in conjunction with constructive food consumption to maximize vitamin intake and usage.

Another incredibly important aspect of eating is the action itself: chewing. Chewing is the cornerstone of the eating process. Without the ability to chew, we would not be able to consume most products available in the world. The current issue most of us face with chewing is that we do not chew enough.

Every organ in our body utilizes energy to execute its function. The stomach uses energy to release gastric acids to break down food into chyme. The small intestine uses energy to absorb nutrients from this broken-down chyme. Our liver uses energy to process these nutrients and metabolize them. And so on.

When we do not chew enough, the particles entering our stomach require more energy to be exerted in order to be broken down properly. Likewise, because the resulting chyme passing into the small intestine is not broken down as thoroughly as it should be, the intestine needs to leverage more energy. And this continues throughout the entire digestive chain.

And what happens when these processes utilize more and more of our body's energy? We end up with less energy for our daily activities. Fatigue skyrockets. Physical performance drops. Reaction time slows. Mood becomes more susceptible to swings. A whole array of negative consequences.

So, what must we do to combat this? Simply chew more! It is recommended we chew our food 32 times before swallowing it.[5] The food entering our esophagus should be mush-like – having lost all its initial texture.

I know this sounds weird, but take these two examples. Firstly, would it be easier to swallow and pass through a rock or soup? Obviously the soup! Why? Because the rock may be too **tough** for our body to handle and could lead to digestive problems. Secondly, would it be easier to swallow and pass through a rock or the same rock crushed up into a dust-like powder? Definitely the crushed rock! It is still the exact same thing – a rock. But because it is **broken down**, our body will be able to process it easier.

Our body needs foods that go in and out the easiest. This is food that is soft when going into the digestive track. You can eat tough food, like meat. Just make sure to chew enough so your body does not have to work overtime 'chewing' it internally for you.

It may seem odd to be talking about eating in correlation with being happy. But it truly is connected. What we eat affects how we physically feel. How we physically feel affects our mental standing. Our mental standing affects our attitudes and reactions. And our attitudes and reactions determine our happiness.

'Healthy eating is a way of life, so it's important to establish routines that are simple, realistically, and ultimately livable'

Horace

SLEEPING

Sleep is a quintessential factor in the quest of happiness. However, sleep itself is not the important factor. It is rest. We can be sleeping, but not be resting – a reason why many of us wake up feeling terrible and have low energy levels throughout the day. So, our quality of sleep is very crucial.

Similarly, the length of sleep is also important. Contrary to public opinion, not everyone needs eight hours of sleep. Traditionally, most people need between seven and nine hours, but some may only need six hours and others may need as much as ten hours of sleep.[6]

The key is not only to sleep an ample amount, but to have consistency of sleep. Sleeping six hours today and nine hours tomorrow may seem like a solid move, as you are making up lost hours from today. But, regularity of such a variance in sleep actually causes decreased energy overall in the long run.

Our bodies are wired to crave consistency. That is why habits are hard to build but also hard to break – whether good or bad. Sleep is no exception.

Circadian rhythm is our body's internal consistency regulator for sleep cycles. It follows a 24-hour pattern, which is why you often feel tired around the same time on most days.

Being consistent in the time we sleep, how long we sleep and how we sleep is crucial to keeping the circadian rhythm system in good condition. Having a healthy rhythm is key to improving sleep quality, increasing energy levels, improving cognitive performance and regulating hormones.[7]

So, let's start fixing our sleep.

Start by finding your own optimal sleep level. Spend 1 week sleeping around the same time each day – choose a time that works best for your schedule, whether that be 8pm if you have to wake up early or 11pm if you have to stay up late. Similarly, wake up each morning with no alarm – allow yourself to sleep as much as you can every single night. Analyze how long you slept each day and how you felt in the morning and throughout the day.

The day that your optimal sleep level falls under is not the day where you wake up with the most energy. Rather, it is the day where your energy is most consistent throughout the day. You should feel similarly capable in the evening as you did in the morning.

Once you find this day, establish your very own sleep schedule based on this day's sleep duration. Try going to bed every night at the same time. It doesn't have to be perfect. But aim to give no more than a one-hour variance among days. Similarly, aim to wake up every day at the same time. Waking up earlier is better, for, as many successful corporate executives state, we can get a jumpstart on our tasks for the day.[8]

Within this, there is also the crucial element of how we sleep. Most of probably fall asleep scrolling our phones, listening to music with earbuds or headphones, or other entertainment-consuming ways.

The issue is, the moment we are devoid of these habits, we are usually unable to fall asleep easily. These crutches cause lower sleep quality and also increase sleep latency (the time it takes us to fall asleep).[9] So the first step in changing how we sleep is to cut out all un-natural elements. We should be sleeping with nothing in our hands or ears.

Likewise, it is also beneficial to sleep in optimal temperature conditions. Sleeping between 60- and 68-degrees Fahrenheit will allow us to fall asleep faster and often helps us sleep with a higher quality of rest. The exact ideal temperature varies from person to person, but the best temperature is the one where you feel cool but not cold, such that you can fall asleep without shivering.

Lighting is another crucial aspect for sleep. Exposure to traditional white light and device blue light before we go to sleep causes our body to be tricked into thinking it is daytime. Instead of these sources, we should be using soft light with colors like orange, red and yellow for two to three hours before we sleep. These colors help promote sleepiness and release melatonin in the body,[10] a hormone which helps us wind down.

Similarly, when using devices, we should use night shift mode to reduce exposure to blue light.

The last and most crucial element of healthy sleep relates to food and water. Sleeping on an empty stomach is most ideal. Large meals before sleep can cause poor rest and can also disrupt hormones.[11] Likewise, our spine's position during sleep often prevents organs from functioning to capacity, and can cause food digestion issues. Thus, we should avoid eating for one to two hours before sleeping.

However, adequate hydration is crucial to procuring undisturbed sleep. We should drink ample water 20-30 minutes prior to going to bed. This is key for waking up feeling rejuvenated.

Following all these steps will lead us to sleep with restfulness and fulfillment. It will allow us to wake up with high energy and maintain it throughout the day.

'Sleep is that golden chain that ties health
and our bodies together'

Thomas Dekker

A mental trick that can aid sleep quality is this: **Sleep like it is the last time you will ever sleep. And wake up like it is the first time you have ever woken up.**

Following this trick wholeheartedly causes us to sleep more deeply and with more meaning, which indirectly causes more vivid dreams and provides a higher quality of rest. Similarly, this trick will allow us to wake up with more energy by making our mind eager to tackle on the challenges of the day.

A physical trick to promote better sleep is sleeping on our back – military style. While it may take a few days to get used to, this position causes less tossing-and-turning through the night, leading to a better quality of sleep and in turn providing more energy to use during the day.

When we sleep better, we have more energy. When we have more energy. We are more cognitively capable and less emotionally influenceable by the world around us. When our brain is active and our emotions are stable, happiness and well-being come with ease.

EXERCISING

Exercise is an essential component of happiness. Most of us often experience mental unhappiness because our physical state is poor. When we cater to the physical, the mental is easier to work on and may even improve on its own.

Now, exercise is not just working out in the traditional sense – lifting weights, running, push-ups & sit-ups. It encompasses all aspects in which the body is active and not stationary. Walking. Playing sports. Gardening. Dancing. Yoga. Stretching. All these are prime examples of various types of exercise.

The thing with exercise though is that we must be willing to push ourselves. Regardless of what we do, whether it is lifting heavy weights or walking, we must push ourselves to physical tiredness.

When we push ourselves to where our body is physically tired, a whole flood of hormones and neurotransmitters are released. Endorphins for pleasurable well-being.[12] Serotonin for sleep.[13] Dopamine for enjoyable habit building.[14] Adrenaline for energy availability and usage.[15] And so many more.

When these natural chemicals are released into our body, we are not only physically more able but are also mentally more resilient and more capable of living with well-being. For example, dopamine from exercise causes us to feel increased pleasure and happiness. And dopamine also causes us to crave for the source that released it. Because of this, we will, over time, crave to exercise more, which causes more dopamine release, which fuels more happiness. A never-ending cycle.

Moreover, exercise plays a crucial aspect in the other topics mentioned so far in relation to experiencing happiness physically. Adrenaline and improved insulin sensitivity from exercise causes improved metabolism, which helps us utilize food nutrients better. Serotonin from exercise helps regulate mood, sleep and appetite, all of which reduce symptoms of depression.

Again, the most important part of exercise is that we push ourselves. Now, this doesn't mean we should go do what everyone else is doing. We each have our own unique limitations. Our goal should be to break these limitations and not strive to live up to the standards of others.

Exercise is something that is extremely hard to start. The first phase of exercise is not a battle of the physical, but a battle of the mental. If we solidify our mental fortitude and push through this first phase of difficulty, we benefit in the long run through physical improvement, mental empowerment, psychological strength and the resulting happiness that follows.

Exercise is crucial to staying happy. So regardless of how you do it, from walking to dancing, exercise frequently and always push yourself till you cannot anymore. The more we push ourselves today, the more we benefit tomorrow.

'Physical fitness is not only one of the most important keys to a healthy body, it is the basis of dynamic and creative intellectual activity'

John F. Kennedy

MOVING

The last big physical element of happiness is moving. Now, when I say moving, I am not talking about walking, standing or sitting, but rather **how** we do these activities. There are three main factors that go into how we are moving: posture, attitude and breathing.

Posture is simply our physical position when doing all activities. Our posture is primarily a subconsciously controlled activity – our body has a 'natural' posture. The problem is that this natural posture is often times contradictory to what the best posture actually is for our bodies as a whole (muscle, organ and skeletal systems).

The main takeaway from posture is to always be upright, regardless of what we do. Most of us have hunchback from staring at screens and sitting at desks. But this is easily fixable in the way we position our spine and back. Our back should be as straight as possible. But the trick is to not just pull your back up and straighten it, but to pretend as if someone is pulling strings from above connected to your shoulders. This automatically straightens our spine, pulls our shoulders back and puffs up the chest, aspects which all support a healthy posture.

It'll 100% be very uncomfortable for a few days as we start to consciously do this – we have gotten so used to comfort in our posture that anything new will be uncomfortable. But as we actively and consciously practice good posture, it will take over as our new habit.

Posture also refers to how we do tasks, such as going from sitting to standing, lifting weights or heavy objects and other spine contracting/protracting activities. Regardless of what activity it is, the best practice is to keep our back upright. The spine is the central component of our bodies – in the sense that everything in our body relies on its function. Catering to our spine will indirectly cater to all other bodily elements.

When your posture is proper, your bodily processes require less energy, leaving more for you to use throughout your day. More energy means more drive. More drive leads to more success in our tasks. More success leads to improved happiness.

Subsequent to posture, our attitude is also a prime element of moving. We should do all posture related activities with upmost confidence and belief. What I mean by this is that we should literally sit, stand and walk like we can do and achieve anything and everything in this world.

We should do so not with the belief of pride – that we are better than other people – but with the belief of grace – that we are and will continue to be great.

It may seem silly to say and think about, but I want you to recall someone you think is confident and commanding – perhaps a motivational speaker. Now imagine this person slouching while walking or sitting, or moving with their shoulders pushed forward. Would they even exemplify 1% of the confidence they so previously radiated?

It is important to have confidence in moving for two reasons. Firstly, it improves other's trust and belief in you. It gives them confidence about your character and abilities. Secondly, it does the same for you. The more we do something, the more we become it. The more we move with confidence, the more confident we will be.

And when we start experiencing this sense of greatness from our movements, our happiness will subsequently rise as our belief in ourself has risen.

You do not even have to have any confidence to start this. Fake it till you make it. A reporter once asked Rihanna what she does on the days she does not feel confident, fearless or powerful. Rihanna answered "pretend." Even when we do not believe in ourselves, if we act like we do, we will convince others we do and ultimately will slowly start to manifest it internally.

'If I feel confident wearing something, I think it translates in photographs. It changes my demeanor and posture'

Nina Dobrev

The last big element of moving is breathing. I will start off with an example. Which animal do you think will grow up with more energy and strength: a horse that absorbs 50% of oxygen or a horse that absorbs 80% of oxygen, with all other factors the same for both. Without a doubt the 80% absorption horse!

The reason the horse that absorbs more oxygen will live better is because oxygen is the lifeblood of all living mammals. The more oxygen you absorb, the more energy you will have, the more physically capable you will be and the more quickly you can recover.

As a mammal, this context applies to humans as well. The more oxygen we get, the better we can live.

There was a medical event that occurred a while ago. A woman's leg had turned very blue and swollen due to a lack of blood circulation. Doctors agreed the leg was beyond recovery and recommended amputating it so that the effects wouldn't spread and get worse. But one doctor suggested putting the woman in a hyperbaric oxygen chamber – a system which supplies pure 100% oxygen.[16] Within a few hours, the woman's leg started to turn pink and blood was circulating.

'Your body's main source of energy is oxygen. Period'

Belisa Vranich

Oxygen is crucial for our bodies to function. The more we get of it, the better we can function.

Currently, most of us breathe subconsciously. It is a process that is natural and not actively thought about. And while there is nothing wrong with this, we can improve our physical well-being simply by consciously breathing.

What is meant by this is that we must actively, throughout the day, take time to simply breath. Take long deep breaths through the nose and exhale back through the nose. The trick is to go slowly and deep. Repeat this in-and-out breathwork for four to five repetitions five to six times throughout the day. Over the course of one full week, you yourself will see a dramatic shift in your mood, energy and ability to recovery.

Controlling our breath is also just as important. This applies primarily to physically exhaustive activities, such as exercise. When our heart rate goes up during intense activities, blood in our body circulates faster. This is important because blood transports oxygen to our muscles and organs, which is what gives us the energy[17] for such activities in the first place.

It is important to take time/make space to breath in these activities because, if our breathing is not good, less oxygen will be transported through the blood. When less oxygen is transported, we get tired faster, have less energy and will be less capable. Conversely, when we control our breathing and ensure a recurrent fresh supply of oxygen, O_2 is dispersed better throughout the body, which aids our physical capabilities, endurance and recovery.

The easiest way to control breathing is to set aside just three to five minutes every day to meditate. Now, meditation is beneficial for a countless number of reasons, but with regards to breathing, it helps regulate the flow of oxygen throughout the body.

So right after you wake up or before you go to bed, just sit cross-legged on the ground for three minutes. Three minutes is all. Put all your mind's focus on your nose and listen, feel and see how your breath is going in and out. Aim to breathe deep and fully.

And when your mind wanders off your breath to other thoughts, mark those thoughts mentally, set them aside to deal with after and get back to focusing on your breath.

After those three minutes, oxygen will have spread throughout the body, the mind's racing thoughts will have suddenly organized themselves and peace and calmness will have spread throughout us.

Our breathing, postures and attitudes while moving throughout the day dictate our energy. Our energy dictates our capabilities. Our capabilities dictate our mood. And our mood dictates our happiness. Aim to be holistic in accounting for how our lives are lived physically and happiness will simply follow.

PUTTING IT ALL TOGETHER

There was a lot that was talked about in this chapter. You may feel swamped by all that was said. But the truth is, at the core, there is only one factor that determines how we experience happiness in terms of a physical context: **energy**.

Energy is the will of our body. Without energy, we would not be able to live let alone achieve all that we desire to achieve. Maintaining peak energy is crucial to living life fully.

And so, start building energy levels and capabilities by targeting the four sections described: eating, sleeping, exercise and moving. As these areas begin to be developed, the production of energy within our bodies will be enhanced.

With more energy, we will be less inclined to feel physically unable, weak, or stunted – factors which otherwise inhibit our ability to pursue the goals of our lives. And as we feel better physically, we can achieve more and have our happiness levels subsequently rise.

This is the path forward towards experiencing the emotion of happiness the physical way.

So, the next time you feel sluggish, tired, exhausted or anything but ecstatic in the morning, go and stand outside in the sun for 10 minutes. Watch how your entire mood turns upside down and you begin to question why you felt off in the first place. Simply because you got some good-old fashioned vitamin D.

Engross yourself in that which is mother nature. Breathe in fresh air. Tend to your garden. Hug a tree. Take that ant that has been bothering you in the kitchen and put it outside. Witness your negative experience transform entirely into a positive one.

Eat fruits and gain energy. Sleep like you will not wake up tomorrow and wake-up like you were just born. Push the body and build endurance. Breath fully and deeply and feel less tired. Meditate and experience peace and tranquility. Stand straight and command confidence.

When our body is physically active, it is impossible to feel emotionally discontent. Our 'depression' and unhappiness will simply disappear, at the very least for the duration of the activity, but guaranteed for longer if done with consistency.

Our physical bodies are nothing but natural chemical factories. Dopamine. Serotonin. Endorphins. Adrenaline. Histamine. By hacking our system to crave for natural (physical) activities that produce these and other bodily-occurring chemicals, we will begin to lose the negative mental strains that we face.

It is this natural disappearance of negative feelings, attitudes and 'disorders' that will lead to the next part of happiness: sustaining it.

Set The Body free.

'Letting go of what no longer serves us is the first step toward discovering our true selves'

ARG

Chapter 3

Mental Happiness

Let's jump back to the talk of emotional control mentioned at the start of this book. All of us have life goals. Maybe we want to become a successful business owner. Maybe we want to be a good author. Maybe we want to be a strong lawyer. Maybe we want to be a contributor to society.

Regardless of what the goal is, it is likely a big goal. Big not in the sense that it is hard to achieve – which it may be. But big in the sense that where we are right now is far away from where we need to be to achieve it.

The only thing between our goals and us achieving them is action. The action we take towards them. The action that puts us one step forward for every inch we take in the right direction.

The issue most prevalent among a lot of us in chasing our goals is that we simply do not take action. We are all inherently capable of taking action – good action to reach our goals. But the reason we do not is due to one factor: it is difficult.

Why is it difficult? Because it means being and acting different to reach our goals. But being different means feeling uncomfortable. And feeling uncomfortable means uncertainty. And uncertainty means work without guarantee.

And because it will make us feel uncomfortable and the outcome is uncertain, we choose to procrastinate and avoid beneficial action in search of other activities that provide us with immediate gratification.

But the truth is, we procrastinate this way not because we do not believe in our ability to reach our goals. In fact, it is the opposite. Denis Waitley once said "you know if you did it, you'd win. And you'd be better. So I didn't do it so I could be my comfortable self. Next thing I know the opportunity passed. Phew. It felt so good. Just to be me again."

We all know if we tried, we would succeed. But we don't try because we do not want to be and act different to reach our goals. Thus, we avoid uncomfortableness and can stay our 'content' and 'happy' selves.

This is clearly a fallacy. We avoid hard things so we can stay 'happy'. But we also know if we had the things that come from hard work, we would be more happy. An endless loop that consumes most of our existence.

This is known as the fear of success. We all face it. We know we could do it. But we don't because we like how we feel right now. And we are not willing to risk that feeling for an uncertain, better future.

The only reason we face this fear of success is because of one factor. **Our Emotions.** If our emotions didn't dictate our feelings and make us feel uncomfortable, we would strive to achieve all that we could as fast as we could. We would be an unstoppable force.

Take this example. Let's say you were selected to give a speech in front of an audience of 10,000. There is no time limit at all; you can speak for as long or as little as you want. The only rule is, you must go up and speak about something. With our emotions ruling us, a lot of us would likely just plan to go up for a mere one to two minutes, planning so out of fear that we may stumble or say the wrong thing and end up embarrassing ourselves. But imagine if you couldn't mess up. If whatever you said was amazing and inspiring. And nervousness and emotional feelings couldn't control you. In this case, we would certainly plan to speak for as long as we physically could. Because we all have good things to say. The only thing holding us back is fear.

This is all it is. Our emotions dictate our feelings. Our feelings dictate our capabilities. Our capabilities dictate our action. Our action dictates our success. And our success dictates our happiness.

If you have ever done any kind of public speaking before – school presentations, community talks, debates, etc. – you know that the scariest part is not the speaking itself. It is the moments before you speak. Your heart is racing. Mind is all over the place. You are freaked out. But the moment you start speaking, the words start flowing out like water falling from a waterfall – ever flowing and continuous.

All hard work is like this. It is always scary until we start. But the moment we do, it all fades. It may not feel easy. But it definitely does not feel hard. It is just work. Progress to be made.

It would be nice if emotions didn't give us fear – if all we could feel were warm feelings.

But the world doesn't work this way. Winners and losers are decided purely on ability. Ability not to feel great and thus achieve success. But to feel horrendous and still achieve the same success. Very few successful people in the world have reached their heights without struggling and going through emotionally turbulent times. When it happened along their journey, why would we think it wouldn't or shouldn't happen on ours?

It is time to break the cycle and take action. Ignore all feelings but good ones. Let your self be fully immersed in all that you do. Take in the good, bad and the ugly. But, let all feelings come to be one. Set on this path and your life will change monumentally with every step you take.

'You can choose courage, or you can choose comfort. You cannot have both'

Brené Brown

But what does setting on this path actually mean and look like? What steps do we have to take to be on it? I break it down in two categories: Giving up and taking on.

Giving up has to do with all the things we must let go to get where we need to go. It may mean leaving our circle of friends and entertainment venues behind – any and all activities we physically do that are not consistent with our goals. But it doesn't stop here.

We must also give up some of our emotions. This brings me back to the emotional control talked about in the first chapter of this book. Remember, emotional control doesn't mean suppression of emotions. It means not dealing with them.

Emotions are all made up. It's a fugazi. It's a fugazee. It's a wazee. It's a woozee. It does not exist. It is fairy dust.[1] Emotions are simply what we feel. And everything we feel is simply **our reaction** to our experiences. So, to control our emotions, we must simply change our reactions.

The first step to doing so is correcting our mindset. A lot of us have what is known as a 'fixed mindset' – a mindset where we do not like change or unknown situations; anything that will 'disrupt' us from our rhythm. But this is simply human nature: we desire the comfort and security we feel in routine.

To overcome this, we must make active effort to switch our fixed mindset to a 'growth mindset'.

A growth mindset is one where we are constantly in pursuit of developing ourself. It is where we are **OPEN** to everything, but also **QUESTION** everything. We are never content with where and who we are currently because we know that, for every second that passes, we can be and do better, regardless of how great or un-great we may be right now.

It is easy to say or think that we already have a growth mindset. But just that belief, that we **ALREADY** have this perspective is proof that, in actuality, we have a fixed mindset. The one with the goal of growth is either so sure their mind is fixed or so scared they it may be that they are constantly keen on always striving to do better and learn more in any circumstance.

When we take this first step of implanting a growth mindset attitude and demeanor within us, we can begin the process of controlling our reactions and subsequent emotions.

The first and easiest way to control our reactions is to switch our language. Change "**I have to**" to "**I get to**". I get to go to work today. I get to go to the gym. I get to get rejected by this person I will ask out later. I get to get a ticket from this cop. Our subconscious is incapable of differentiating between what we say and what we feel. So eventually, what we **SAY** will become what we **FEEL**.

Do not ever say negative things such as 'I am dumb' or 'I am stupid'. Our mind does not know the difference between statements said and actual feelings felt. And so just by saying these things, even if we do not mean them, we will eventually become them. Even if we are stupid or dumb – which, for the record, we are not and never will be – **NEVER** acknowledge or entertain such statements or feelings.

It may seem simple enough to do, but actively watch yourself throughout the day and you may find that, more often than not, you will say things that you do not truly think or feel are true.

Give up any and all negative self-talk. It affects us more than we know. Whenever we make mistakes, do not take them as opportunities to criticize ourselves. Rather use them as events to serve as standards to build off of next time.

Mistakes are hard to deal with – they sting and hurt. Make us feel less than. The key here is realizing we are not our mistakes. We are what we do because of our mistakes. Years after our mistakes, they collect together and form what we call 'an experience.' And experience ultimately guides our actions.

Make mistakes. Just don't let yourself be them. And the key to doing so is changing our language. For when our words change, our emotions change. When our emotions change, our actions change. When our actions change, our capabilities change. Change how you talk to yourself and the capabilities before you will be limitless instead of limited.

'It's not what you are that holds you back,
it's what you think you are'

Denis Waitley

Another way to manage our reactions is to stay absolutely neutral.

Through the winter of 2023 and 2024, I trained to become a d2d salesman. One of the most prominent things they talked about in training was the importance of neutrality. When you are at someone's door trying to make a sale, if you let your emotions control you, nine times out of ten you will lose that sale. For emotions will always get the best of you. But if you steady your mind and stay neutral, ignoring both the good and bad of the situation, you will be able to push past objections and make the sale come through.

Life is the same way. When we have a goal in sight, it is in our best interest to stay absolutely neutral regardless of the situations and experiences that occur on our path to achieving that goal.

Let me give you a scenario to think about. A peak is known as a highpoint and a trough is known as a low point. If we reach a peak feeling, by definition, it means we cannot possibly feel any better – we have reached the top. The only way to go is down – meaning, we will feel worse and worse, relative to the peak. Similarly, if we reach a trough in terms of feeling, by definition, we can only feel better and better, relative to the trough.

This is a viscous cycle. But it is the cycle of life. Reaching a peak means the only way to go is down. And reaching a trough means the only way to go is up. A peak and trough may not necessarily be the highest or lowest points overall, but in the current cycle of where we are, they are the highs and lows.

If we live our life succumbing to these peaks and troughs – that is doing good when we reach peak feelings and doing bad when we reach trough feelings – we will always be taking steps back. We may take two steps forward, but we will also take one step back.

This is where neutrality comes in. Staying neutral breaks these peak/trough cycles of emotion and feeling. Being neutral means, regardless of where you are, you will continue to move forward. Instead of having a cyclical path with ups and downs, you will have a linear path which only goes up.

This doesn't mean you won't fail. You will. All this means is that you will not let the failure determine who you are and what you do. You will be the same regardless. Similarly, when you succeed, you do not let your success fuel any overconfidence or pride. You remain the same as you were before. And who you were before is someone who only has one goal: the pursuit of their dreams.

So, we fail in our quest to receive equity funding for our new business? Do not feel sad or upset, for now we are instilled with the lessons to never make the same mistakes we made this time or to simply do better and try more next time than this time.

We finally reach $100k in revenue for our new business? Do not celebrate [excessively], for we are taking ourselves away from our real goals (ex. $1m in revenue) and **DIMINISHING** our ability to continue forward **by MAKING OURSELVES FEEL CONTENT** with where we are now.

Just stay neutral!

'Your Mind Will Take the Shape of What You Frequently Hold in Thought, For the Human Spirit Is Colored by Such Impressions'

Marcus Aurelius

But obviously, staying neutral forever is simply not ideal nor feasible. For if we do not feel anything in this life, then what is the point of living? The answer to that question is that we should only feel the good stuff. And the good stuff is all centered around happiness. This is where we must start taking on.

Block out the disruptive noise and let in the calming breeze. Focus your mind on all that is well. Feel and express gratitude, for there is more in life to be happy for than there is to be unhappy for. Accept every moment for the beauty it is, for you still draw breath in this very second. Let your mind be free, not captive.

From the moment we are born, every second we are creeping closer to our death. Every second is so darn precious because it is a moment of life we will never, ever get back. And, every second there are a million things we can think about. So why waste our disappearing time thinking and focusing on the bad?

But the question is how can we focus only on good? The answer is so simple. Just choose. Choose to listen to the light and not the dark. See the nice and not the mean. Be the good and not the bad.

When you focus on all that is great in the world, all that you feel will be great. And when all that you feel is great, all that you think will be great. And when all that you think is great, all that you will do is great. And when all that you do is great, all that you will achieve is great.

Great. Great. Great. All is great. See great. Hear great. Spread great. Love great. Lose great. Win great. Fail great. Preach great. Think great. Laugh great. Cry great. Shine great. Do great. Live great. Recognize that all there is in life is greatness. Stay great and grateful!

So, we succeed in our current school tasks? Good, for now we know what we must continue to do to reach higher levels. We successfully launch a new business? Good, for now we have a framework to build off of and improve on.

We fail miserably in our presentation at work? Good, for now we know what we must do differently next time in order to do better. We get rejected by the girl of our dreams? Good, for now we are one step closer to finding the one for us.

Every situation has good in it. The question is, are we open to seeing, accepting and living off of it. If we are, our life will not only transform in terms of what we do achieve. But what we can achieve becomes endless.

Celebrate every single moment in utter joy and happiness, regardless of whether it is inherently good or bad. **EVERY FAILURE OR OBSTACLE IS BUT A NEW PATH TO THE SAME ACTION**.

All that we want in the world is within an inch of our grasp. That inch comes in the form of not what we can achieve, but what we think about us achieving everything in the world. The more good we think, the more good we believe we are capable of. Your mind becomes what it deliberates. So deliberate that of goodness, greatness and happiness.

Everything will improve if we start making an effort **NOW**.

'If any external thing causes you distress, it is not the thing itself that troubles you, but your own judgment about it. And this you have the power to eliminate now'

Marcus Aurelius

Once we have changed our language and mindset, we must start to begin spreading more love. But what is love?

Most people define love as a feeling. A deep feeling of care for someone or something else. A google search defines it as "an intense feeling of deep affection."[2] But love is not a feeling, it is an action.

We can say we love someone or something, but if we do not take actions that demonstrate so, how much love really is there? Let me give an example. Let's say you love your dog. You tell everyone you love it. You think it yourself. But if you do not spend time with your dog, tell your dog you love it or do other actions that convey that love, do you really love it?

When we say we love something, we must be ready to defend it. Defend it not with words, but with our actions. Show through actions how much that love means to us and how deep it really goes. For action is the only true measure of feeling. There is a saying that says "actions speak louder than words," and this applies to all elements of life, but especially our feelings.

But love is not simply for people or things. It can be for all of life itself. Think about it. The odds of any one of us being born exactly as we are is one in a nonillion (10^{30})! There was a greater chance for you to have never existed than there was for you to be as you are right now.

The miracle of creation is one that we should be in awe of. Life is so unbelievably beautiful. We have trees so green that we cannot look any direction without seeing them. A sky so blue we could spend all day staring at it. Breeze so gentle to the skin and warm to the ears it brings us peace. Water so abundant it surrounds us in every direction.

When thinking about creation, what is there to not be in awe of? Everything is literally so, so, so extraordinarily beautiful. And how can we not be chronically infatuatedly in love with all of that?

By recognizing the immensity of what creation is, we should start building love for it. But remember, love is not a feeling, it is an action. So, we must act with love for all of creation.

Let me share what I have been doing personally. When I wake up every morning, I open my window and stare at the sun for a few seconds. When I walk outside for the first time, I close my eyes and smell the air and feel the breeze. When I eat my meals, I stare at the food and think of where it came from. And before I go to bed, I stare into the night sky and see the endless stars in our galaxy staring right back at me.

Loving creation means taking time for it. Appreciate the beauty of the world and everything in it. But creation is not just nature. It is people. We are all of creation. So, love people as well!

We see someone with a nice haircut? Compliment them. We see people working outside in the hot sun? Cheer them. You see a person with a nice outfit? Let them know. We see someone with a cool car? Go with curiosity and ask them questions about it. After all, if we were in their positions, **wouldn't we want someone to do the same for us?**

Loving somebody doesn't have to mean things such as you would do anything for them or you would 'die' for them. It can be as simple as appreciating the fact that there is another human being around you who breathes the same air you do. And that appreciation is shown through action in the form of giving complements, committing kind gestures and expressing gratitude.

It is important to love and spread love because love is the cornerstone of happiness. Even if you fail in achieving all that you desire to and live every day with struggle, if you have love, you can still be eternally happy.

As we begin to spread love throughout the world, love begins to spread within us. This love leads to us being consumed by goodness. Goodness is not only a quality of having virtue and being good but also the action of creating happiness and spreading good for ourselves and those around us.

The more goodness we create in the world, the more goodness will come back to us.

> 'In the end, the love you take is equal to the love you make'
>
> *The Beatles*

> 'Only A Life Lived For Others is a Life Worthwhile'
>
> *Albert Einstein*

This ideology reflects that of the ethical dimension of Karma. If you do not believe in Karma, that is ok. Just read the following with a receptive mind.

I want you to recall an instance in your life where you behaved inherently bad towards someone – maybe a peer, friend, or family member. Recall how you felt in that moment.

Now, recall how you felt in the days/weeks/months following that event. I can almost 100% guarantee that you felt or went through unfavorable times, were experiencing bad events, or just all out in general were not doing good.

Now, I want you to recall an instance in your life in which you know you did a good deed for someone or something, whether it was saving someone's life or simply putting an annoying ant/spider outside instead of killing it. Recall how you felt in that moment.

Now, recall how you felt in the days/weeks/months following that event. In this instance, it is almost certain that these proceeding periods were ones where you triumphed and were thriving.

This is the concept of Causation Karma. What we give is what we get. Give anger and hatred and anger and hatred will come back to us. Give love and joy and love and joy will come back to us. Forgive those who trespass us just as we wish to be forgiven for the ones we trespass. Just as mother nature operates in cyclical seasons and patterns, so do our minds, bodies and spirits.

You don't have to even believe in 'karma' to see the truth in these statements. I am confident everyone reading this has felt and lived bad when engaging in bad actions and has felt and lived good when engaging in good actions.

This is crucial because we can quite literally change our life and experiences simply based on what we put into the world. All we have to do is believe. Believe we can change and we will.

I will jump back to what I spoke about earlier in this chapter. The mind does not know the difference between what we say and what we feel. So eventually, what we say will be what we feel.

But saying things doesn't just mean verbal "speakage." What you say in your mind is the factor above all. It is the ruler of your capabilities. The way it works is as follows.

What we think influences what we feel. But what we verbally say influences what we think. They go hand in hand. If we do not say anything verbally, but speak in our minds, what we speak in the mind will be what we feel. But if we are constantly verbally talking and preaching something, that thing will be what we mentally think about and subsequently will be what we feel.

If what we speak is goodness, what we think will be good and what we feel will be good. Then, because what we feel is good, we will spread good around. And when we spread good, good will come back to us.

'The person who does wrong, does wrong to themselves. The unjust person is unjust to themselves – making themselves evil'

Marcus Aurelius

And it all starts with belief. Conor McGregor, after his 13 second KO of Jose Aldo in UFC 194, said "If you can see it here and you have the courage enough to speak it, it will happen." Belief is all we have. When we truly, with every cell in our body, believe something can happen, it will.

Belief is a determinant of action in our minds. If we didn't believe in our mind we would get a good job, would we waste our time going to college? If we didn't believe we could get a promotion at work, would we actively work harder to get it?

This may seem like we have hope, but it is not just hope. There is no such thing as hope without some degree of belief. It is because we believe, even if the size of a poppy side, something can happen that we have hope it will. Because if we didn't believe, we wouldn't have hope.

Hope without belief is lack of faith. It means nothing. For if we hope something will happen but don't think it can, it will almost never happen. It is ok to doubt. Doubt is what gives us and helps us keep reason in our mind. But doubt doesn't mean disbelief. **Do not let it lead to disbelief**.

But do not stop at belief. Turn that belief into expectation. Expect things to go your way. Deepak Chopra, a new age spiritual leader, went onto The Oprah Winfrey Show to talk about the importance of belief and expectation. He handed Oprah a string with a washer tied to the end and told her to hold the string from her finger tips with the washer hanging straight down. He then told her to imagine in her mind the washer swinging back and forth. And it started to swing physically. And then he said imagine, in the mind, it going in circles. And it started swirling physically.[3]

This is what expectation is. When we expect something to happen, it has a great chance of actually happening. And expectation stems from belief. The more we believe, the more we expect.

Expecting is good. But never, ever make the mistake of relying on your expectations. Things often do not go our way, even when we expect them to. And if we over-expect something only for it to not be delivered, it will fuel greater disappointment than if we never expected it in the first place. And that greater disappointment will cause a series of shocks in our ability to believe, which will be detrimental to our drive to succeed in the short run.

So simply, believe, hope and expect good things to happen to you and for you. But do not rely on these things. Have back-ups to fall on in the case things turn out opposite to expectations.

'For truly, I say to you, if you have faith like a grain of mustard seed, you will say to this mountain, 'Move from here to there,' and it will move, and nothing will be impossible for you'

Jesus | Gospel of Matthew, Chapter 17, Verse 20

Our minds are an ever-changing organism. They adapt on a daily basis to what we experience and feel. It is beyond important to treat our minds with care in order to develop them into the potential they are capable of.

I like to use the metaphor of an egg. Our minds are currently an egg sitting in boiling water. Slowly, they become harder and harder in the inside. And eventually, they become so hard their form won't change any more – a hardboiled egg. Do not let your mind come to this state. Instead, crack the egg. Break off your existing knowledge, experiences and feelings. With that cracked egg, we can make scrambled eggs, fried eggs, omelets and so much more. The possibilities are endless. Just if we crack that which is holding us back.

Cracking our pre-conceptions doesn't mean disregarding them. It simply means, we are open to new conceptions. Always stay open-minded and receptive. Constantly take on that which you know will be better for you. Let go of the things you know are pulling you down.

It will always seem hard. That's why so few succeed in doing it. But remember, it is only hard until we start. And once we start, it is not easy nor hard. It simply **is**. Every step forward is one step closer. Every action taken is one less action to take.

Stay neutral or only be happy. The choice is yours and yours alone. Nobody and nothing in this life can make us sad, bring us down, make us happy, or bring us up.

It is all what you allow your mind to receive that depicts what your experience will be. You can let what others say or do and the circumstances around you affect you and who you are. Or you can simply not deal. Not deal with anything that has the potential to hold you back.

Indulge in the bad, and the bad we shall undergo. Rein in the good, and the good we shall flourish in.

In this chapter, we have deliberated primarily about what we must think and do to guide us in enacting action to reach our goals. The reason for this focus is because our ability to reach our goals and dreams is ultimately what depicts our happiness.

Nobody wants to get old and look back having wished they did something or avoided something. This just causes unhappiness. Which is why it is of upmost necessity for us to constantly strive to reach our long-term objectives. For they will pave the path for bringing upon happiness on ourselves.

That is not to say you must achieve these ambitions. But what you must do is make the effort. For it is that – taking the chance – that depicts whether or not you will look back with pity and anguish or gratefulness and joy.

As we actively make the effort to master our mindset into always looking to grow, change our reactions to only seeing and always spreading joy and love, and constantly strive to live for the greater good, we can allow ourselves to be receptive to experiencing that is what is True Happiness.

Life is constantly in motion and never stays the same. We must grow resilient in adapting to this change by making the efforts above.

It is 100% a lot. But doing only 50% of this will give you 50% happiness. Doing 100% of it will let you be 100%. Everything you need in this life is built within you. Most of us just have trouble accessing that which we seek to experience.

Don't be troubled by trouble.

'As Long as There Is Breath in Our Lungs, Our Story is Still Being Written'

Bart Millard

'Meditate often on the swiftness with which all that exists and is coming into being is swept by us and carried away. For substance is like a river's unending flow, its activities continually changing and causes infinitely shifting so that almost nothing at all stands still'

Marcus Aurelius

'To get what we've never had, we must do what we've never done'

ARG

Chapter 4

Sustainable Happiness

As you have read, I am sure you've felt overwhelmed. It is not obvious on the surface just how broad and deep happiness actually is. But it is truly a holistic encompassing of all aspects of life. And to be one with happiness, we must aim to encompass all these aspects.

Before fully diving into how we can sustain happiness, I would like to share a few stories of prominent individuals across world cultures. The first person I would like to talk about is Jesus Christ of Nazareth.

Jesus Christ is a man who was born and lived free of sin. He lived a life that most people today would consider 'horrific'. Constantly opposed by those around him. Oppressed by the religious leaders of the time. Beaten and tortured by Romans. And, ultimately, brutally murdered through crucifixion at the young age of 33.

But despite all these negative outcomes he faced in life, Jesus never changed. Even while he was dying on the cross, he cried out to the Father (God), saying 'forgive them for they know not what they do'[1] – a message he preached throughout the entirety of his life.

And Jesus structured his life this way based on one underlying principle: love. Today, people say 'Jesus loves you'. But no single phrase can convey the immensity of the love Jesus truly has.

Let me give an example. If Jesus' mother, Mary, was in peril danger and the only way to save her was to kill his neighbor (fellow man), Jesus Christ would not do it. Regardless of the pain he knows he would feel for losing his mother, he would never dare to lift a finger against his fellow man.

Why? Because Jesus Christ loved equally and deeply. He loved his neighbor the same way he loved his mother. He saw everyone as the same – a creation in the universe. Jesus knew the shame, guilt, or sense of wrongness he would feel for killing his fellow man would be far more permanent than the despair he would feel for losing his mother.

Why would this feeling be greater than the loss? Because despair can be overcome. Overcome with memories of joy and happiness. Overcome with experiences and recurring emotions of love. However, sense of wrongness and guilt can rarely be overcome, because no matter what we do in this life time, we can never have not done that which we wish we never had done.

Regardless of whether you believe Jesus Christ is God or not, the message is still just as prominent. Even if he is only a man, he is a man willing to spread nothing but love across the world and give his life for it even when facing the most torturous methods of death.

The reason why Christians believe Jesus takes away sin is not only because of their faith in him as God. But because the one who truly understands the teachings and love of Jesus Christ will aim to emulate this spirit of Christ in their own life. The concept of becoming Christ-like.

The message of Jesus Christ is clear. Spread love into the world. Why? Because, as the golden rule says, we must do to others as we would have them do to us. It is about giving what we want to be given. And all we as humans want is love, in a multitude of forms.

I am sharing this message because this is the way of living. We are all brothers and sisters, having descended from the same forefather and foremother.

We must live not only for ourselves and our direct family, but for our family across the world. Your neighbor. Your doctor. Your boss. We are all one big household.

We should even live for that which we consider nature. Plants. Animals. Insects. Everything! For we have **all** originated from the soil of our planet and to the soil **all** of us will eventually return.

'Hatred stirs up conflict, but love covers over all wrongs'

King Solomon | Book of Proverbs, Chapter 10, Verse 12

'A new commandment I give to you, that you love one another: just as I have loved you, you also are to love one another'

Jesus | Gospel of John, Chapter 13, Verse 34

'And now these three remain: faith, hope and love. But the greatest of these is love'

Apostle Paul | First Epistle to the Corinthians, Chapter 13, Verse 13

'And over all these virtues put on love, which binds them all together in perfect unity'

Apostle Paul | Epistle to the Colossians, Chapter 3, Verse 14

'Above all, love each other deeply, because love covers over a multitude of sins'

Apostle Peter | First Epistle of Peter, Chapter 4, Verse 8

Jesus spoke about love. Love is the bridge between all actions and happiness. To have love, there must be some element of happiness underlying the love. For if there was none, there was no love.

Take this example. We love somebody extremely deeply. So much so that we smother them. But we also know that our smothering is holding them back – maybe in terms of their goals. It is then up to us to let them go, for if we don't, then that is not love but selfishness. And letting go doesn't mean having or feeling only good stuff. It means sacrifice and pain. But we sacrifice and take on this pain because we know our loved ones would be happier in the distant term without us than with us. And this, that they will be happy because of this action, is what makes us happy, even if it makes us sad.

To be truly happy, we must always, and I mean always, actively wish for and cause happiness in all those around us.

Think about a time in childhood, during school perhaps, when you and all of your friends and/or classmates were all laughing and having a fun time, say at recess.

Now imagine this same experience, but instead of everyone being happy and laughing, it was just you and everyone else was sad or gloomy.

Would this experience feel even 1% as amazing and as joyous as before?

Spreading happiness is all about spreading love, for it is love that brings about happiness to us all. We can be most happy when all those around us are happy. Self-centered individual happiness may feel good. But that feeling fades faster than snow melting in the summer sun.

Causing happiness doesn't mean putting other's well-being over yours. Because if your well-being isn't good, how can you help make other's well-being good? It is also not about weighing interests about whose is more important either.

Causing happiness is about doing good for all. And there is a 'selfish' reason for us to do so! Doing good for others means doing good for you, for what you put out always comes back in. So do good for others for your own well-being.

And doing good simply means spreading love. Spreading love through all the actions talked about in chapter three and so many more. If you would have something happen to you that you believe would be good for you till you die, it almost always means doing it for somebody else will also result in something good happening for them.

And spreading love is most effective through non-material means. Compliments. Gestures. Attention. These are all factors that skyrocket happiness. Whereas if you do gestures like giving gifts and money, while the action can reciprocate love, it is not actually love itself. Material spreading of love, like self-centered happiness, is fading. It cannot last, for our expectations will be raised to desire for these material things, and when we do not get them, we will feel no love.

That is not to say do not give material things. Make the giving thoughtful. If your child has always had an interest for learning an instrument, take them to classes. Connect them with good individuals to guide them. But above all, make it known why you are doing the action. You are doing it because you know it means a lot to them – that is love.

But love, happiness and goodness do not always mean everybody benefits. If something is good for me, but not you, it is not good. If something is good for you, but not me, it is not good. If it is not good for society, but good for me, it is not good. But, if it is not good for me, but good for all those around me, it is good.

Actions which are good for most, even if bad for you, are usually good. And, while it may not be actively seen, it **will** cause you happiness, which ultimately benefits you. For the one that constantly takes for themselves will eventually find they have nothing left to take and will be filled with emptiness. But the one who constantly gives will find they will be given more at the end of it all.

But remember, that doesn't mean only prioritizing others. We must be in a stance of well-being to even be able to care for others. The trick here is we should all aim to live with the bare minimum we can and aim to give more than we have.

If we all lived this way, imagine how much more love and goodness there would be in the world.

Someone will always make the argument "but if I do it and others do not, how will that be beneficial? There won't be any meaningful impact." To that, I say. Global change always starts with the one person who has the courage to change before all others.

Be that 1st Person.

'Whoever Is Happy Will Make Others Happy'

Anne Frank

'Happiness Quite Unshared Can Scarcely Be Called Happiness; It Has No Taste'

Charlotte Bronte

The second example of an individual I would like to share is the life of Rama. Rama was a prince to-be king of an ancient kingdom (Kosala) in India. His step-mother wanted her own child to be crowned king instead, and thus used a vow made by Rama's father, the current king, to send Rama away.

Rama's father did not want to give in, as he desired to see Rama on the throne. But Rama himself went to his father and convinced him to oblige to the vow. Rama declared it is a sin and mistake to break that which we promise.

Rama then willingly went into exile for 14 years, during which he faced horrific situations. His wife was kidnapped. His brother almost lost his life. He was constantly on the move responding to these situations.

Rama ended up having to kill Ravana, the ruler of Lanka and kidnapper of Rama's wife, to put an end to these atrocities.

Even though it was the righteous thing to do (protect his wife), Rama knew it was wrong for him to kill a king, a leader of a nation. And so, to atone for this act, he himself willingly went into penance for an entire year.

The reason I am sharing this story about Rama is because of his righteousness. Rama knew it was right for him to save his wife, but he also knew it was wrong of him to take a life.

The righteousness of Rama and sinlessness of Jesus lives within all of us. We all have a desire for selfish, short-sighted sin. But we also have the tools to overcome this desire by acting with righteousness aimed at doing good.

We all know what is right and wrong. Most of us just choose to ignore it. It is that gut feeling that may be intense or faint, but it is there regardless. Listen to this feeling, for it will guide us to living lives that bring us true happiness.

To understand whether actions are good or bad, it is helpful to refer to ethics. There are three major types of ethical frameworks: deontology, consequentialism and virtue ethics.

Deontology has to do with morality of and reasons for actions. Deontologists believe in a set of rules that should be followed no matter the circumstance.

Consequentialism has to do with the outcomes of actions. Consequentialists believe the best actions are ones that maximize the utility (well-being) of all.

Virtue Ethics has to do with personal character. It is about becoming the type of person who lives virtuously, with traits like wisdom and compassion, and acting the way this type of person would act.

While all three offer different approaches to ethics and morality, the one I like to focus on is virtue ethics. I am fond of virtue ethics for several reasons. Take these two examples –

Example one is one went over in a law class I attended: a murderer is trying to kill John. John runs to your house and asks if he can hide there. You say yes and tell him to hide inside. The murderer comes knocking and asks if John is there. You can be honest or lie.

Example two is a classic conundrum used in ethical and philosophical debates called the Trolley Problem: you are a trolley captain. You are heading towards five people tied down to the tracks in front of you. There is another track to your left which has one person tied down. You can switch to the left track, killing the person tied down on it, but saving the five people on the other track, or stay on your current course.

For the first example, under deontology, one must follow all rules regardless of the circumstance. One of those rules is often having integrity: not lying. But if you are honest to the murderer about John hiding in your home, then the murderer will come and kill him. Under virtue ethics, one must act as they would act with good character. The one with good character aims to be compassionate and courageous and thus would lie to the murderer to save John's life.

In the second example, under consequentialism, the consequentialist would switch to the left tracks, killing the one person and saving the five people. Their reasoning for so would be because this scenario maximized the overall utility – saved the largest number of people. The virtue ethicist may similarly switch to the left tracks, but their reasoning for so would be drastically be different. The one with virtue ethics principles would weigh all factors, such as whether the people were children, whether there were alternative actions, how each choice may affect the broader community, how this would affect their own character and so on.

These examples are of course selective, chosen to show how virtue ethics looks past the unfeasible strictness of rule-following deontology and inhumaneness of quantitative-based consequentialism. But virtue ethics has short comings too, specifically focused on circumstances where virtues may clash, such as being loyal to friends and acting with integrity to other people.

The reason however that I like virtue ethics in particular is because it is about the development of the self – bringing yourself to become and acting like the best version of you. It is about acting with goodness in the heart. Weighing all factors in every scenario and doing what one would while thinking about all effects to anyone and everyone.

But we must not stick to one framework or another. The truth is, the most ethical actions switch between and lie in all three frameworks. They are not mutually exclusive or mutually exhaustive and can work hand in hand.

That which is good and bad can also be determined by listening to the heart. There was a study done last year and published this year (2024) in which neuroscientists studied the human heart and found it had 40000 cells called sensory neurites (neurons) which are vital in memory transfer and play a role in cognition and mood regulation.[2]

The heart is critical in our thinking ability. Just thinking about it logically, the heart affects physical state. The physical state affects our feelings. Our feelings affect our mood. Our mood affects our thoughts. And our thoughts affect our actions and capabilities. But it is deeper than this.

The heart also quite literally thinks on its own. It can learn, remember, sense and feel. And when we train our heart to act with virtue, we can rely on our heart to guide us in the right direction even when our mind cannot. And we train our heart through the actions we take.

The first steps to take in changing our actions is to base them on some sort of ethical rationale, such as using the ethical decision-making frameworks described before. Another great first step is to avoid short-sighted traps.

When I say short-sighted traps, I am in fact referring to sin. Now, I am not here to lecture you on the morality of sin and why we should avoid it. I prefer to call them 'traps' because that is essentially what they are – actions which offer short-term gain by sacrificing our long-term vision and goals.

We all know in every moment what is good and bad and what we should do and should not do. And yet, we choose the contradictory choice more often than not. A prime example that comes to my mind is procrastination – we know deadlines are around the corner, but we choose to wait until the absolute last second to start because we believe the work can still be done. And while the work can probably still be completed, its quality is absolutely not going to be anywhere near where it could have been had we given it more time. In addition, the more we procrastinate, the more likely it is we will also convince ourselves that the actions we should be taking are not important or needed, and thus avoid doing them all together.

Avoiding these traps is how we prevent ourselves from developing a short-sighted mentality that will slowly eat away at us and our well-being.

But what exactly are these traps? There are seven primary actions to avoid: lust, gluttony, envy, sloth, wrath, greed, and pride. These are traditional Christian teachings of traps/sin, but they reflect values from other cultures like Hinduism, which advocates abstinence from the six enemies of the mind, and Buddhism, which talks about the five poisons.

Regardless of the culture, these actions are simply human flaws. By addressing these flaws, we can be free from that which is holding us back. Each of these traps offer pleasure in the short term. But we mistake this pleasure for happiness, which it is not.

Lust is the trap of our deep desires. It refers not only to the lust for people, but for the lust of all things in this material world. Lust cultivates five of the other six traps, acting as a foundation for them all.

To overcome lust, we must desire nothing. Nothing is what we came into this world with and nothing is what we leave this world with. Anything in between is temporary and fleeting. Desire nothing. When you desire nothing, you will find you receive everything.

Desiring nothing is not the avoidance of having goals – it means **not being attached** to them. Because when we are attached, pain will inevitably follow because all material things eventually come to an end. Avoiding attachment means we strive for goals, but are indifferent to achieving them or not – our virtues and mindset remain the same regardless.

Gluttony is essentially over-indulgence. Taking more than our fair share. It refers not only to food but all aspects of life. Greed is the root of gluttony.

To overcome gluttony, we must aim to give more than we get. Every second of the day, aim to provide more than you are provided with. Love more than you are loved. Forgive others even when they do not forgive you.

Living this way will result in us leading fruitful lives that bring us more happiness than indulging in gluttony. For what we give always comes back to us.

Sloth is our desire to have everything but not work for anything. It is our entitled-ness and belief that we deserve all in the world. It is the reason we feel envious when we see others with that which we don't have and desire to possess.

To overcome sloth, we must realize everyone has what they have for a reason. The rich man is rich for a reason. The poor man is poor for a reason. What will your reason and outcome be?

Are you going to let yourself be defined by your current situation or past failures, using them as an excuse to avoid action? Or aim to try more and fail more so that you may succeed just once?

Wrath is hatred, resentment and envy wrapped up together. Wrath is what we feel when we believe we are wronged. It is what we feel when we believe others have what we 'deserve'. Its roots are self-pride and self-righteousness.

To overcome wrath, one must forgive. When you experience anger, the only person you are hurting is yourself, for you are literally poisoning your own blood stream.

Love others the way we wish to be loved. Forgive those the way we wish to be forgiven. Afterall, other than our own selfishness, what makes us think that there is a justified reason for our wrath?

Envy is tied to every trap mentioned so far. It is a part of desire. Our desire for what others have and our desire for them to not have what they have. Our desire to be greater than and above others.

Greed proceeds envy, leading us to actively act only in our interests and not in the interests of humans as a whole. It makes us selfish and self-centered. Greed destroys all virtue.

To overcome greed and envy, we must remind ourselves we will always get what we deserve. When we are greedy and envious, we will become the victim of greed and envy. But if we are not attached to anything, we will find we already have everything.

And lastly, Pride. Pride is at the forefront of all these traps. Pride is the originator of all sin. Pride is the belief that we already are above everything. That we deserve all, simply because we are better.

Remember. **Nothing is what we came into this world with. Nothing is what we will leave with.** In between, we are nothing. And when the sun engulfs our planet, everything will be nothing. **Nothing is all there is**.

Pride is our inner evil. A ruthless master responsible for all things terrible in the world.

Pride fuels Lust. Lust fuels Sloth. Sloth fuels Envy. Envy fuels Wrath. Wrath fuels Greed. Greed fuels Gluttony. Gluttony fuels Pride.

And the cycle repeats. Break the cycle to be liberated.

Destroy Your Pride Before Your Pride Destroys You

Basing our lives and actions on virtue (ethical behavior) and avoiding the seven traps is how we can start the flourishing of happiness.

These two elements are of upmost importance. For without them, there will always be a sense of longing within us. Nothing will ever be enough and we will always have this deep-rooted feeling of emptiness.

Destroying sin and having virtue fills this empty space in us. It acts as the foundation of our life, providing us a framework to live and base actions off of.

All the steps mentioned so far, from the physical paths of happiness to the mental paths of happiness, are steps that alone can provide happiness, but not <u>sustainable happiness</u>. That is, it is not happiness that will forever stay without constantly increasing effort.

Virtue and sinlessness are what turn these actions into a lifelong sustainable pursuit of happiness. Happiness we will feel even when only mildly embarking on the various paths to happiness. For we will be filled with bliss and contentment.

I am not saying we have to be perfect. Being sinless is something I have only known Jesus to be. And always upholding virtue is something I have only known the greatest stoic philosophers to do.

But what we do have to do is **try**. Just try. You never know what you are capable of until you take the very first stride.

So, take it.

'Dig Deep Within Yourself, For There is a
Fountain of Goodness Ever Ready to Flow if You
Will Keep Digging'

Marcus Aurelius

'Perseverance Is the Bridge between The Life
You Have to The Life You Want'

Uknown

'You have proof in the extent of your wanderings that you never found the art of living anywhere — not in logic, nor in wealth, fame, or in any indulgence. Nowhere. Where is it then?

In doing what human nature demands. How is a person to do this? By having principles be the source of desire and action. What principles?

Those to do with good and evil, indeed in the belief that there is no good for a human being except what creates justice, self-control, courage and freedom, and nothing evil except what destroys these things'

Marcus Aurelius

Chapter 5

A Personal Anecdote

So far, I have talked about what you and we all should be doing to experience happiness. I would now like to take a moment to share why I have chosen to talk about this topic.

Since my childhood, I have been on the pursuit of happiness. No matter what I did, I always did it because I believed it would bring me a great deal of happiness.

In my early years, I would leap at the opportunity to participate in activities. I would strive to win competitions. I got in debates all the time just to explain why I was right.

But slowly, over time, I began to become more and more self-centered. My pursuit of happiness turned into the chase for instant gratification. I wanted everything and I wanted it now.

It all seemed okay on the surface. I was doing solid in school. Had outstanding extra-curriculars where I achieved immense success. Excelled across various personal interests.

But inside I felt emptier and emptier as the days went on. My mood started to swing back and forth more and more. I attained less and less incremental happiness the more I had achieved things. I was never able to stay still and appreciate all I had and did in life.

And it came to a breaking point. I was full on depressed. Isolated myself from friends and family. Started hanging out with the wrong crowds. Picked up bad habits. My life was thrown into a spiral.

This continued for a few years. A cycle which I tried to break numerous times but ended up back doing all the things I knew I shouldn't have been. A life centered on short-sighted sin.

That was until the summer of this year, 2024. On June 3rd 2024, I decided to make a change.

You see, I knew the life I had been living was dragging me down – mentally and materially. I was falling behind in all that I wanted to do and achieve. And as I reflected more and more on the promises I made to myself when I was a child, I realized I would not bring one of those dreams to reality if I kept on my current destructive path.

And that realization forced me to destroy my life as I knew it and hit the reset button. And from that day on, the 3rd of June 2024, I have never been the same.

I started off by cutting out all my bad habits. All the traps I was falling into on a daily basis. I knew they were wrong; they were bringing me down and causing me tremendous downfall academically, financially and emotionally. So, they had to go.

The next step was cutting out all the things I was doing simply out of compulsive desire. Spending excessive time with friends. Watching hours and hours of Netflix every day. Eating disastrous foods full of processed and detrimental content. Staring at my phone for over seven hours a day. It all went to the trash.

I spent the next two weeks resetting my life. I did not pick up any new tasks or start new activities. I simply got rid of all that I was doing that wasn't actively making me a better person or bringing me closer to my childhood dreams.

The first day was beyond all difficulty I could imagine. I had terrible cravings for all the things I cut. I quite literally would pick up my phone every five minutes just out of compulsion. It was the toughest mental battle of my life. And this continued for the first seven-ish days.

Around the eighth day, my compulsiveness had decreased. My brain's old sources of dopamine were cut off and my brain finally knew it could not rely on those venues.

At this time, I began to increase the activity of all the good things I had already been doing, which primarily was just going to the gym. I went from working out just two to three times a week to working out every day. And not just working out, but pushing myself to the absolute peak of my capability. I continued with this for the next week or so.

Around the 15th day, I began to feel 'normal' again. My brain was active with desire to try out new activities and craved new dopamine sources. My energy was through the roof and I felt more capable and determined than I ever had before in my life.

It was at this point that I began to take up new activities. And these were centered around reading, learning, personal development, food consumption, physical action, sleep and faith.

I started to read in all ways I could, focusing in on self-development books. I read the personal writings of Marcus Aurelius, Meditations. This led me to stoic philosophy, through which I learned about virtue and good character and began my journey of understanding the proper principles to build my life around.

This took me to developing. Developing myself in all aspects of life – physically and mentally. I began to study and learn the best practices at the gym to understand how I could lift better. I studied proper posture techniques and ways of stretching to assist in living a more mobile life. I embarked on a journey of mental development, applying the principles of stoic philosophy into my day-to-day life and spending several hours a day to work on my craft – strategy formulation.

My journey of development led me to the importance of eating, through which I transformed what I was consuming. I cut out all sources of added sugar – cookies, cakes, bars, etc.

– caffeine – for me, soda - and overly-processed foods. These were all foods and drinks I learned were causing me immense mental swings throughout the day by directly influencing my energy levels. I also transformed my diet to always start and end the day with only fruit, eat more fruits and veggies, eat more protein and aim overall to eat foods that nature provided as opposed to that made by man.

My consumption journey dramatically changed my energy levels by making them stable and consistent regardless of the day. This in turn let me perform better physically at the gym and throughout the normal course of my day, leaving me less fatigued. It also made me mentally sharper, more capable and, most importantly, exponentially more driven.

Subsequent to all this, I also changed my sleep. With the level of physical activity I was undertaking, rest was of crucial importance. And so, I began to sleep as early as possible and without an alarm. This let me fully engross myself in sleep, which gave me deeper and more quality rest. And, fun fact, when I made all these physical changes, I saw more muscle, strength and endurance growth than I ever had before.

The last, and most life-changing, thing I did was take on faith. During my zealous undertaking of reading – which included not only books and articles but also news and current events – I came across religion over and over again. So, I decided to explore every major faith in detail and understand the principles of each.

Within the first few days, I felt a connection to God – a connection I hadn't felt since my childhood. And as I read and read, this connection got stronger and stronger. To this day, my relationship to the LORD, my God, grows stronger by the day. Every second I feel closer to God. Every second I feel more loved.

I am sharing this about my faith because this was the final piece of the puzzle that absolutely transformed my happiness. Never before, in my 19, almost 20, years of life, have I ever been this happy. I feel a sense of security I never had. I am at peace with life and all the challenges I have and will face. I feel blissful in every cell of my body.

But it wasn't all sunshine and rainbows. Within a few months, I found myself slowly giving in to the pleasures I thought I left behind. It started out innocently – letting myself watch a TV show because it was religion-based. But soon I found myself back falling into the traps I fought so vigorously to give up.

This continued for weeks and weeks, and finally came to an end when I realized my compulsion for my old life did not outweigh my desire for a new one.

I sit here writing this text almost six months after I initially published this book – making an amendment because I want people to realize what I learned.

It was made clear to me that life is not a straight and linear path. It has ups and downs and turns. What is constant however is struggle.

I used to hear the phrase "the struggle is our salvation." And these words have never been more true for me than right now. You see, no matter what good or bad you do in life, struggle and challenges will always come.

What's important is to realize that who we are is not the bad events or obstacles we face in life. Who we are is what we do because of these roadblocks.

I now know that no matter what temptation or challenge comes to me in my life from here on out, I can and will always get through it.

Simply through blind faith. Believe and it will happen. Know and it will come to pass.

I did not want to write this book to talk about any particular religion, as my intention is to not to alter your religious beliefs. But I cannot in good conscience let this book be re-published without taking a moment to talk about my Lord and Savior, Jesus Christ.

From birth, I was a Hindu and was fully immersed into learning all there was about the various and vast realms of Hinduism's sects – from the dualist beliefs of Madhvacharya to Adi Shankaracharya's non-dualist Advaita Vedanta philosophy.

But that all changed when I listened to a video on YouTube of Jesus preaching the Sermon on The Mount. The first time I watched this video, I burst out in tears. For the love I felt through hearing his words was a love that surpassed even the most immense and ever-unconditional love I constantly feel from my closest beloveds.

Even today as I replay the Sermon on The Mount, tears consume me. Because I have known since childhood the life I am meant to be living. But never once have I actually made the effort to live it the way I know I should be. He came and lived it for me, without a spec of an error. That is how I know he is my Salvation.

I am not asking you to go out and immediately follow Jesus Christ. But I am hoping you take just ten minutes out of your day at any point you can – during a commute, at the gym, in the bathroom, etc. – to watch a video of Jesus preaching the Sermon on The Mount. Just ten minutes – less than 0.7% of all the time in a day. These ten minutes just may change your life the way they changed mine.

Since that day several months ago, the 3rd of June 2024, my life has never been the same. Not only am I truly happy for the first time in my life, but I am more capable, more motivated and closer than ever before to realizing all my childhood dreams. And I know that no matter what challenges I face in life, through faith and unwavering determination, I can get through it all.

A phrase I like to use for those that think about this journey is the following. The first week is hard. The second week is a little easier. The third week feels great. And the fourth week becomes habit.

All the changes I have made so far are ones I made during the first four weeks of my transformation. And they are all ones that I have stuck with and expanded on since then.

In these few short months, I have achieved more than I had in the prior 19.5+ years of my life.

And it all started with the first change.

'Adapt what is useful, reject what is useless, and add what is specifically your own'

Bruce Lee

'A pessimist sees the difficulty in every opportunity; an optimist sees the opportunity in every difficulty'

Winston Churchill

Chapter 6

A Daily Life

So, when you wake up tomorrow, wake up in absolute excitement. Fill you heart with awe in being blessed with another day of life. Feel the ever-gushing energies of the universe circling throughout you. Wake up and <u>be awake</u>.

Once you arise, first pray. It is okay if you are not religious or do not believe in God. Just pray. You can pray to the universe. Express gratitude for waking up today. Fill your heart with gratefulness. This will set the tone for the day.

Faith is crucial because it is what gives us purpose in life. All other things are fleeting because they can be physically achieved. But faith is a never-ending quest into the unknown. <u>Have Faith</u>.

After you pray, sit down with a notebook and write down your goals. They can be short- or long-term goals. Maybe write down what you hope to accomplish in the day – any tasks you want to do. Or maybe go broader. Write down what you want to accomplish 10 years down the line. Writing down goals helps us remember them. And when we remember them, action follows through much easier.

After you have written down your goals, sit on the floor and meditate for a bit – just three to five minutes. During this time, only breathe through your nose and focus on that breath. Feel and experience the air going in and out. Try not to deviate the focus.

When other thoughts rush in – and they will – set them aside to deal with after. The more you focus on one single thing – your breath – the more calm, collected and composed you will feel after the three to five minutes.

Following this brief meditation, get some food in your system. Eat only healthy items for this very first meal. Try to base it solely on fruits – especially oranges, bananas and melons. Fruits give us sustainable energy. They burn up the fastest in the body but give energy that lasts the day. Starting with fruits sets you up with prime energy levels and a healthy mood.

Post meal, immerse into your daily hygiene routine. If you can, take a cold shower. Cold showers wake you up by rushing adrenaline (energy) throughout the body. They are perfect to help us remain more motivated and capable throughout the day. If you cannot take a purely cold shower, just try ending with cold water (last 30 seconds). This will have a very similar effect.

Cold showers are especially effective in the winter. Let me explain the science. Warm showers raise the body temperature. Cold showers reduce body temperature. In the winter, it is already cold outside. When you take a hot shower, your increased body temperature will make you feel even more cold outdoors because your body has to make a larger jump down to reach the outdoor temperature. But, with cold showers, because your body temperature is already lower than normal, your body will make a smaller jump down to reach the outdoor temperature. So cold showers will make you feel less cold in the winter.

Also get in the habit of having a full oral routine after the shower. Most of us probably just brush every day – skipping flossing. But flossing keeps our teeth and gums healthy and strong. And who wants to lose their teeth? Also aim to use a 'tongue scraper' – a metal tool that scrapes against the tongue. The tongue is a prime spot for bacteria to build up. These scrapers help get rid of that bacteria, which helps us have better smelling breath and a healthier mouth.

After your hygiene is over, spend five minutes reading something. It can be anything – a book, news articles, etc. Just read something before starting the day. Reading is the best way to get the mind into the mental state of processing thought.

Once you have finished all these things, then begin your day, whether that is school, work, or a mix of both. And when you are doing these things, give them your all. It is easy these days to feel unmotivated – maybe we don't get paid enough or just do not care much about what we are doing.

But you must not give 100% for your employer's or school's sake, but for your own sake. Giving your all gives us a sense of satisfaction that is unmatched. Even if we fail, knowing we gave it our all is what fuels future drive and determination and prevents regret.

So always aim to give whatever you are currently doing 100% - 100% effort, 100% focus, 100% dedication and 100% care.

Once you finish your daily tasks – work, school etc. – take some time for yourself. Do whatever you want – read, watch something, walk around. But, most importantly, keep it short. The more we prolong this stage, the less we will be able to accomplish after. It is important to take time for ourselves to avoid getting burnt out. Extending that time, even by short amounts like 15 minutes, may not seem like much. But over the course of several days, weeks and months, it adds up to whole days we end up wasting. Prevent this by allocating yourself 'me' time and sticking to just that time.

After your break, dive into the development of the self. Do something every day to progress to your long-term goal. For example, if your goal is to start your own business, spend one to two hours every day just learning some relevant skill for business – like sales, marketing and finance. Doing something every day towards your goal, even if just for a few hours, puts you miles ahead of everyone else in the race. You may not be able to see your progress quantitatively, but these behind-the-scenes actions propel you to new realms of success. The last major tasks you do every day should be catered to your craft.

Between all these things throughout the day, you are of course eating meals. Before each of these meals, while you have the food in front of you, express gratitude. Pray to God or the Universe and fill your heart with thankfulness for being blessed with food – an item that seems so abundant in the world, yet so few have access to. And while you eat, put your phone and any devices away. Focus on the food and only the food. Think of where it came from and how it was made. This will cause you to experience a feeling of gratitude. For example, if you are eating spaghetti, think of how the spaghetti came about from raw wheat. It started from something that grew in the ground. And it was slowly processed into dough. And from dough into long strands. And from long strands into the dried spaghetti most of us buy from the supermarket (sorry Italians!). Think of how the farmer or harvester went about this process and the time and care they used. You, without a doubt, will end up smiling and feeling beyond blessed.

At this point, your day is pretty much coming to an end. As we started the day off with a routine, it is just as important to end in a similar way. Your last meal should always be with fruits – for they will burn the fastest during sleep and help prevent stomach problems like bloating and cramping. After your meal, have a hygiene routine again. Maybe shower again and definitely brush your teeth and rinse your mouth.

After hygiene go back to your goalbook (goals notebook). Read what you wrote earlier. If it was a daily goal, think of how much of the goal you achieved that day. If it was a short-term goal, think of how much progress you made that day. If it was a long-term goal, think of what you did today to bring you closer to achieving it. This act of reminder helps bring our goals closer to our hearts, which is a step needed to achieve them.

Finish reviewing your goals and have this be the third last thing you do before going to bed. The second last thing should be prayer. Express your faith to God or the Universe and show gratitude for having lived another day. The more you express gratitude, the more your heart will be filled and the more your character will be developed.

The very last thing you should do is get into bed. Don't sleep just yet. Instead think about the possibility of you never waking up tomorrow. Think about how you would want to sleep today knowing that you will not wake up again. And then sleep on that thought – aiming to achieve the best sleep you ever had because it may be your last. <u>And sleep</u>.

Following such a schedule throughout the day, over the course of a few days, will cause your virtues to develop and your happiness to rise. It is a slow path, but a consistent one. And consistency is the fastest way to <u>always</u> get what you want.

These days aggregate into months. And the months aggregate into years. And one day, you will wake up and look back and will not be able to recognize the person you once were.

Changing your life is not some big, drastic event. It is a series of minute-by-minute decisions on an every-day basis that combine to propel you to realms and levels you have never dreamed of.

Consistency is the only secret ingredient.

'Take up one idea. Make that one idea your life; dream of it; think of it; live on that idea. Let the brain, the body, muscles, nerves, every part of your body be full of that idea, and just leave every other idea alone. This is the way to success...'

Swami Vivekananda

Chapter 7

Ending Remarks

Absorbing this information may and will make us feel burdened. Happiness is the most difficult thing to start experiencing. No one ever said the journey will be easy. But once we start on this path, leaving it feels impossible.

<u>Starting is hard</u>
<u>Developing is easier</u>
<u>Continuing is easiest</u>

And it is through this consistency that we will begin to experience new means, adventures and capabilities like never before. It's the small things that make the big impacts.

Listen to this book's message not from your mind, but from your heart. For the mind is aggressive, but the heart is receptive.

As Bruce Lee once said, "Empty your mind. Be formless. Shapeless. Like Water." Water takes the shape of that which it is in. And so shall you.

Let mother nature into your heart. A force that tells the birds when to migrate and the flowers when to bloom. So shall it speak to you.

Few will understand. But the one's that do will be truly transformed.

I will leave you all with one final thought.

Would you rather live only one more year, but have it be the most blissful and joyous year of your entire existence?

Or would you rather live another hundred years, but exactly how you have been living?

The best part is, you do not have to choose.

Make this life the happiness you seek to experience.

It is all in your head, after all...

Life is a Game for Everyone. And Love is the
Prize

Avicii

With Sincerity,

    Anish Reddy Gaddam, Happiness Enthusiast

Cited Works

CHAPTER 1

[1] Merriam-Webster. (n.d.). *Happiness*. https://www.merriam-webster.com/dictionary/happiness

[2] Schulz, J. (2015, November 16). *What does a smile say?*. MSU Extension. https://www.canr.msu.edu/news/what_does_a_smile_say

CHAPTER 2

[1] Scheer, R., & Moss, D. (2011, April 11). *Dirt poor: Have fruits and vegetables become less nutritious?*. Scientific American. https://www.scientificamerican.com/article/soil-depletion-and-nutrition-loss/

[2] Cronkleton, E. (2024, January 19). *Why Is Vitamin B Complex Important and Where Do You Get It?*. Healthline. https://www.healthline.com/health/food-nutrition/vitamin-b-complex

[3] Moore, M. (2022, November 6). *How Vitamin C Supports a Healthy Immune System*. Academy of Nutrition and Dietetics. https://www.eatright.org/health/essential-nutrients/vitamins/how-vitamin-c-supports-a-healthy-immune-system

[4] Mayo Clinic Staff. (2023, August 10). *Vitamin D*. Mayo Clinic. https://www.mayoclinic.org/drugs-supplements-vitamin-d/art-20363792

[5] Cirino, E. (2020, March 20). *How many times should you chew your food?*. Healthline. https://www.healthline.com/health/how-many-times-should-you-chew-your-food

[6] WebMD Editorial Contributors. (2022, August 22). *How much sleep do I need?*. WebMD. https://www.webmd.com/sleep-disorders/sleep-requirements

[7] Bryan, L. (2024, March 15). *Circadian rhythm.* Sleep Foundation. https://www.sleepfoundation.org/circadian-rhythm

[8] Ross, E. (2018, May 14). *Is waking up at 4am really the secret to being a successful person? how to wake up early morning.: Virgin.* Virgin.com. https://www.virgin.com/about-virgin/latest/waking-4am-really-secret-being-successful-person

[9] AlShareef S. M. (2022). The impact of bedtime technology use on sleep quality and excessive daytime sleepiness in adults. *Sleep science (Sao Paulo, Brazil), 15*(Spec 2), 318–327. https://doi.org/10.5935/1984-0063.20200128

[10] Summer, J. (2023, September 13). *What color light helps you sleep?.* Sleep Foundation. https://www.sleepfoundation.org/bedroom-environment/what-color-light-helps-you-sleep

[11] Desai, D., Momin, A., Hirpara, P., Jha, H., Thaker, R., & Patel, J. (2024). Exploring the Role of Circadian Rhythms in Sleep and Recovery: A Review Article. *Cureus, 16*(6), e61568. https://doi.org/10.7759/cureus.61568

[12] Professional, Cleveland Clinic Medical. "Endorphins." Cleveland Clinic, 1 May 2024, my.clevelandclinic.org/health/body/23040-endorphins.

[13] Portas, C M et al. "Serotonin and the sleep/wake cycle: special emphasis on microdialysis studies." Progress in neurobiology vol. 60,1 (2000): 13-35. doi:10.1016/s0301-0082(98)00097-5

[14] GoPractice. "How Product Habits Are Formed and What Dopamine Has to Do With It." GoPractice, 8 Nov. 2022, gopractice.io/product/how-product-habits-are-formed.

[15] Verberne, A J M et al. "Adrenaline: insights into its metabolic roles in hypoglycaemia and diabetes." British journal of pharmacology vol. 173,9 (2016): 1425-37. doi:10.1111/bph.13458

[16] Johnson, Anne. "Oxygen Treatment at Duke Saves Girl's Leg From Amputation." WRAL.com, 24 June 2011, www.wral.com/story/9769443.

[17] "Functions of Blood: Transport Around the Body." NHS Blood Donation, www.blood.co.uk/news-and-campaigns/the-donor/latest-stories/functions-of-blood-transport-around-the-body/#:~:text=When%20the%20red%20blood%20cells,on%20oxygen%20to%20make%20energy.

CHAPTER 3

[1] Scorsese, Martin. The Wolf of Wall Street. Paramount Pictures, 2013.

[2] Definition of Love - Google Search. https://www.google.com/search?q=Definition+of+Love&oq=Definition+of+Love&gs_lcrp=EgZjaHJvbWUyBggAEEUYOdIBCDUxMDdqMGoxqAIAsAIA&sourceid=chrome&ie=UTF-8

[3] OWN. "The Oprah Winfrey Show: Conversations with Oprah: Deepak Chopra | Full Episode | OWN." *YouTube*, 24 Oct. 2023, https://youtu.be/QMjGA5dpre0?si=vZFpNAjGyz4-SZVm

CHAPTER 4

[1] English Standard Version Bible. (2001). ESV Online. https://esv.literalword.com/?q=Luke+23%3A34

[2] Tendulkar, Mugdha et al. "Clinical potential of sensory neurites in the heart and their role in decision-making." Frontiers in neuroscience vol. 17 1308232. 13 Feb. 2024, doi:10.3389/fnins.2023.1308232

Simply Be

www.ingramcontent.com/pod-product-compliance
Lightning Source LLC
Chambersburg PA
CBHW051345040426
42453CB00007B/418